African American

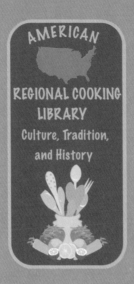

AMERICAN

REGIONAL COOKING LIBRARY

Culture, Tradition, and History

African American

American Indian

Amish and Mennonite

California

Hawaiian

Louisiana

Mexican American

Mid–Atlantic

Midwest

Northwest

New England

Southern

Southern Appalachia

Texas

Thanksgiving

African American

Mason Crest Publishers

Philadelphia

Mason Crest Publishers Inc.
370 Reed Road, Broomall, Pennsylvania 19008
(866) MCP-BOOK (toll free)
www.masoncrest.com

First Edition, 2005
13 12 11 10 09 08 07 06   10 9 8 7 6 5 4 3 2

Library of Congress Cataloging-in-Publication Data

Sanna, Ellyn, 1958-
  African American / compiled by Ellyn Sanna.
      p. cm. — (American regional cooking library)
  Includes index.
  ISBN 1-59084-610-9
  1. African American cookery—Juvenile literature. I. Title. II. Series.
  TX715.S14524 2005
  641.59'296073—dc22

                      2004016729

Food images prepared by Theo's Southern Style Cuisine, Johnson City, New York.
Recipes contributed by Rosa Waters.
Produced by Harding House Publishing Services, Inc., Vestal, New York.
www.hardinghousepages.com
Interior design by Dianne Hodack.
Cover design by Michelle Bouch.
Printed and bound in the Hashemite Kingdom of Jordan.

Contents

Introduction   6–7

African American Culture, History, and Traditions   8–11

Before You Cook

· safety tips   12–13

· metric conversion table   14

· useful tools   15

· cooking glossary   16–17

· special African American flavors   18

African American Recipes   19–65

Further Reading   66

For More Information   67

Index   68–69

Biographies   70

Picture Credits   71

Introduction
by the Culinary Institute of America

Cooking is a dynamic profession, one that presents some of the greatest challenges and offers some of the greatest rewards. Since 1946, the Culinary Institute of America has provided aspiring and seasoned food service professionals with the knowledge and skills needed to become leaders and innovators in this industry.

Here at the CIA, we teach our students the fundamental culinary techniques they need to build a sound foundation for their food service careers. There is always another level of perfection for them to achieve and another skill to master. Our rigorous curriculum provides them with a springboard to continued growth and success.

Food is far more than simply sustenance or the source of energy to fuel you and your family through life's daily regimen. It conjures memories throughout life, summoning up the smell, taste, and flavor of simpler times. Cooking is more than an art and a science; it provides family history. Food prepared with care epitomizes the love, devotion, and culinary delights that you offer to your friends and family.

A cuisine provides a way to express and establish customs—the way a food should taste and the flavors and aromas associated with that food. Cuisines are more than just a collection of ingredients, cooking utensils, and dishes from a geographic location; they are elements that are critical to establishing a culinary identity.

When you can accurately read a recipe, you can trace a variety of influences by observing which ingredients are selected and also by noting the technique that is used. If you research the historical origins of a recipe, you may find ingredients that traveled from East to West or from the New World to the Old. Traditional methods of cooking a dish may have changed with the times or to meet special challenges.

The history of cooking illustrates the significance of innovation and the trading or sharing of ingredients and tools between societies. Although the various cooking vessels over the years have changed, the basic cooking methods have remained the same. Through adaptation, a recipe created years ago in a remote corner of the world could today be recognized by many throughout the globe.

When observing the customs of different societies, it becomes apparent that food brings people together. It is the common thread that we share and that we value. Regardless of the occasion, food is present to celebrate and to comfort. Through food we can experience other cultures and lands, learning the significance of particular ingredients and cooking techniques.

As you begin your journey through the culinary arts, keep in mind the power that food and cuisine holds. When passed from generation to generation, family heritage and traditions remain strong. Become familiar with the dishes your family has enjoyed through the years and play a role in keeping them alive. Don't be afraid to embellish recipes along the way – creativity is what cooking is all about.

African American Culture, History, and Traditions

African American cuisine is often referred to as "soul food." Soul food is soothing and comforting; it is a rich, warm link between people, tasting of home and heritage. It feeds more than the body—it feeds the soul. Soul food is a uniquely American cuisine—but to fully understand these recipes you must also understand the traditional foods of Africa, where soul food has its deepest roots.

When the earliest African Americans arrived in North America, they were already familiar with many common American foods. Grains, legumes, yams, sorghum, watermelon, pumpkin, okra, and leafy greens had all been found for millennium on the African continent. Eggplant, cucumber, onion, and garlic are also believed to be African in origin. Other foods were not native to Africa, but culinary historians believe that toward the beginning of the fourteenth century, European explorers introduced their own food supplies into the African diet. Foods such as turnips from Morocco and cabbage from Spain would play an important part in African cuisine—and in African American cuisine as well.

Meat was rare, so the average African ate mostly a vegetarian diet, though seafood often appeared in stews served with a starch. Okra and native peppers were used as seasoning and salt as a preservative. Africans cooked in boiling water, and they steamed food in leaves. They also fried foods in palm oil or vegetable butters; some ingredients were smoked for flavoring and others thickened with nuts and seeds. Africans also made rice dishes and created fritters. The flavors of these long-ago dishes can be tasted in today's soul food.

The first African Americans were brought across the Atlantic against their will. They brought virtually no physical possessions with them—but they still managed to keep hold of something of far more value: a cultural legacy slavery could not destroy. Stripped of their rights as human beings, these long-ago African Americans managed to hold on to their dignity and their creative fire. They kept their ancient and rich heritage alive through song and prayer, story and dance . . . and through cooking.

With strength and resiliency, the early African Americans adapted to their new lives in a strange and unfriendly land. They took terrible circumstances and inferior foods—the leftovers and table scraps from their white masters' tables—and made the best of them. The tastes and

techniques of Africa flavored the meager ingredients they were allowed—and out of this dark and tragic period in American history came a unique cuisine that demonstrates the cultural victory of a courageous group of human beings.

So cook yourself some soul food! You'll find these recipes continue to offer simple comfort and hearty nutrition.

Before you cook...

If you haven't done much cooking before, you may find recipe books a little confusing. Certain words and terms can seem unfamiliar. You may find the measurements difficult to understand. What appears to be an easy or familiar dish may contain ingredients you've never heard of before. You might not understand what utensil the recipe calls for you to use, or you might not be sure what the recipe is asking you to do.

Reading the pages in this section before you get started may help you understand the directions better so that your cooking goes more smoothly. You can also refer back to these pages whenever you run into questions.

Safety Tips

Cooking involves handling very hot and very sharp objects, so being careful is common sense. What's more, you want to be certain that anything you plan on putting in your mouth is safe to eat. If you follow these easy tips, you should find that cooking can be both fun and safe.

Before you cook...

- Always wash your hands before and after handling food. This is particularly important after you handle raw meats, poultry, and eggs, as bacteria called salmonella can live on these uncooked foods. You can't see or smell salmonella, but these germs can make you or anyone who swallows them very sick.
- Make a habit of using potholders or oven mitts whenever you handle pots and pans from the oven or microwave.
- Always set pots, pans, and knives with their handles away from counter edges. This way you won't risk catching your sleeves on them—and any younger children in the house won't be in danger of grabbing something hot or sharp.
- Don't leave perishable food sitting out of the refrigerator for more than an hour or two.
- Wash all raw fruits and vegetables to remove dirt and chemicals.
- Use a cutting board when chopping vegetables or fruit, and always cut away from yourself.
- Don't overheat grease or oil—but if grease or oil does catch fire, don't try to extinguish the flames with water. Instead, throw baking soda or salt on the fire to put it out. Turn all stove burners off.
- If you burn yourself, immediately put the burn under cold water, as this will prevent the burn from becoming more painful.
- Never put metal dishes or utensils in the microwave. Use only microwave-proof dishes.
- Wash cutting boards and knives thoroughly after cutting meat, fish or poultry — especially when raw and before using the same tools to prepare other foods such as vegetables and cheese. This will prevent the spread of bacteria such as salmonella.
- Keep your hands away from any moving parts of appliances, such as mixers.
- Unplug any appliance, such as a mixer, blender, or food processor before assembling for use or disassembling after use.

Metric Conversion Table

Most cooks in the United States use measuring containers based on an eight-ounce cup, a teaspoon, and a tablespoon. Meanwhile, cooks in Canada and Europe are more apt to use metric measurements. The recipes in this book use cups, teaspoons, and tablespoons—but you can convert these measurements to metric by using the table below.

Temperature
To convert Fahrenheit degrees to Celsius, subtract 32 and multiply by .56.

212°F = 100°C
(this is the boiling point of water)
250°F = 110°C
275°F = 135°C
300°F = 150°C
325°F = 160°C
350°F = 180°C
375°F = 190°C
400°F = 200°C

Liquid Measurements
1 teaspoon = 5 milliliters
1 tablespoon = 15 milliliters
1 fluid ounce = 30 milliliters
1 cup = 240 milliliters
1 pint = 480 milliliters
1 quart = 0.95 liters
1 gallon = 3.8 liters

Measurements of Mass or Weight
1 ounce = 28 grams
8 ounces = 227 grams
1 pound (16 ounces) = 0.45 kilograms
2.2 pounds = 1 kilogram

Measurements of Length
¼ inch = 0.6 centimeters
½ inch = 1.25 centimeters
1 inch = 2.5 centimeters

Pan Sizes

Baking pans are usually made in standard sizes. The pans used in the United States are roughly equivalent to the following metric pans:

9-inch cake pan = 23-centimeter pan
11x7-inch baking pan = 28x18-centimeter baking pan
13x9-inch baking pan = 32.5x23-centimeter baking pan
9x5-inch loaf pan = 23x13-centimeter loaf pan
2-quart casserole = 2-liter casserole

Useful Tools, Utensils, Dishes

colander

cookie sheet

peeler

pie plate

roasting pan

saucepan

skillet

Cooking Glossary

baste To moisten at intervals with a liquid.

dash A few drops.

diced Cut into small cubes or pieces.

dredge Drag or toss meat lightly into a seasoning mixture; be sure to cover the entire piece of meat.

marinade A seasoned sauce in which food is soaked to enrich its flavor.

marinate To allow a food to soak in a seasoned sauce.

minced Cut into very small pieces.

parboil To boil briefly as a preliminary cooking procedure.

pinch An amount that equals less than 1/4 teaspoon.

simmer Gently boil, so that the surface of the liquid just ripples gently.

stock A liquid in which meat, fish, or vegetables have been simmered, used as a base for gravy, soup, or sauce.

toss Turn food over quickly and lightly so that it is evenly covered with a liquid or powder.

Special African American Flavors

brown sugar

cayenne pepper

cornmeal

garlic

salt pork

nutmeg

onions

paprika

African American Recipes

Barbecue Sauce

Good with chicken, spare ribs, or pork.

Ingredients:

2 tablespoons melted pork fat or bacon grease (you can use melted butter)
1 large onion, **minced**
2 tablespoons cider vinegar
¼ cup brown sugar
2 teaspoons mustard
1 teaspoon celery seed
¼ teaspoon cayenne pepper (optional)
1 cup ketchup
3 tablespoons Worcestershire sauce
4 tablespoons lemon juice
1 cup meat **stock**
½ cup beer or white wine (optional)

Cooking utensils you'll need:
measuring spoons
measuring cups
mixing spoon
saucepan

Directions:

Heat the grease or butter in a large heavy saucepan over medium heat, and then brown the onion, stirring frequently so it doesn't burn, for about 5 minutes. Add the remaining ingredients and bring them to a boil. Turn down heat to low and *simmer* uncovered for twenty minutes.

Tips:

Baste meat only during the last 15 or 20 minutes of grilling, or the sauce is likely to burn and the spices' taste will change and become bitter.

This sauce can also be used as a *marinade*. Soak the meat in the sauce for at least 2 hours before cooking; then wipe off the excess sauce, and grill, basting during the last 20 minutes as above.

If you want to make barbecued meat during the winter, try baking the meat in a 350-degree oven. First *parboil* the meat for 15 minutes to get rid of the extra fat. Then bake in a roasting pan covered with aluminum foil for 45 minutes. Pour barbecue sauce over the meat, cover, and continue to bake for another hour, until the meat is tender and pulls away easily from the bone.

If you don't have stock on hand, you can use canned beef broth.

If you choose to use beer or wine in your barbecue, the alcohol will cook away, leaving only the flavor.

African American Food Traditions and History

The earliest African Americans combined their cooking traditions with European foods to create a unique cooking style all their own. Southern plantation owners lived far apart, isolated from one another—so when they did get together, they entertained on a large scale. Huge outdoor meals with barbecued meats were popular—and of course, African Americans were the ones who did the cooking.

After the Civil War brought freedom to the Southern blacks, African Americans still faced many problems. Black communities worked together to help one another, and if a neighbor faced a financial crisis, everyone chipped in to help. Rent parties were social affairs held to raise funds for a family who didn't have enough to pay the landlord. Everyone brought barbecue and other "soul foods," all for sale for a modest price that would accumulate enough dollars to get the family by for another month. The rent parties often turned into block parties, and the sweet smell of barbecue would fill the streets.

African American Food History

During the cruel dark days of slavery, African Americans lacked the freedom to express their creativity through drawing or writing. But the white man could not take away their music—nor their cooking. Black cooks were supremely creative. Like their West African ancestors, they used six basic cooking techniques: boiling in water, steaming in leaves, roasting in the fire, baking in the ashes, toasting beside the fire—and frying in deep oil. It is this last technique that has endured to this day.

Fried Chicken

Ingredients:

cut-up chicken
salt and black pepper (to taste)
dash of garlic salt or powder
dash of onion salt or powder
1 cup flour for every 6 pieces of chicken
2 tablespoons paprika for every cup of flour
2 cups vegetable oil

Cooking utensils you'll need:
large cast-iron skillet
large plastic bag

Directions:

Remove the fat from the chicken pieces, and then rinse. Put flour, spices, and chicken pieces in a plastic bag and shake, so that the chicken is evenly covered. Heat oil in the skillet over a high burner, and then put the chicken in the hot oil. Cook for five minutes on each side and then turn. Keep turning every five minutes until the chicken is golden brown. Lower the heat to medium and cover, allowing the chicken to steam for about a minute. Then use a fork to remove chicken pieces from the oil and drain on a paper towel.

Tips:

Be very careful when using hot oil not to spill any on your skin or the burner. Chicken will pop and snap a lot while it's frying, so use gloves and splatter screen to protect yourself.

You can use a cooking thermometer to determine when the oil is hot enough (375 degrees Fahrenheit)—or you can put a single drop of water in the oil. If it snaps and crackles, the oil is ready.

When using a skillet or frying pan, always remember to turn the handle so that it doesn't stick out where a younger brother or sister might grab it. When using a cast iron skillet, the handle can become very hot, so be careful not to touch it with your bare skin.

Barbecue Pork Sandwich

Preheat oven to 300 degrees Fahrenheit.

Ingredients:

1 four-pound pork butt or five-pound pork shoulder
1 tablespoon brown sugar
1 tablespoon flour
1 tablespoon dry mustard
1 teaspoon salt
1 teaspoon black pepper
1 teaspoon paprika
1 teaspoon red pepper (optional)
1 teaspoon garlic powder (or 1 clove garlic, **minced**)
1 teaspoon chili powder
½ medium onion, chopped
½ cup water
½ cup vinegar
½ cup broth from the cooked meat or chicken **stock**
1 tablespoon lemon juice

> *Cooking utensils you'll need:*
> *measuring cups*
> *measuring spoons*
> *saucepan*
> *roasting pan*
> *meat knife*

Directions:

Place all ingredients except for the meat in a heavy saucepan and *simmer* for 20 minutes over low heat, stirring frequently. Remove from heat, cover, and set aside.

Place the pork in a shallow roasting pan with 2 cups water. Cook in the oven for about 3 hours until very tender. Remove the meat from the bone, taking out any fat. Chop the fat very thinly, so that the meat looks shredded.

Put the meat in a refrigerator container, pour the sauce over it, and let it *marinate* in the refrigerator for 12 to 24 hours. Reheat on the stovetop in a saucepan or in the oven or microwave. Serve hot on buns.

Tip:

Barbecued pork sandwich is traditionally eaten with coleslaw.

African American Food Tradition and History

African American food is well-seasoned. Black pepper and chili powder are found in many of their dishes.

Chili peppers from the Caribbean and peppers from West Africa were important elements of the slave trade; both were thought to prevent dysentery, an unpleasant disease that causes cramping and diarrhea. Also, in the days before refrigeration, spices improved the taste of meat that might be slightly "off" after being stored in the hot Southern summers. No wonder then that African Americans developed a taste for hot and spicy food!

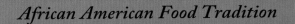

African American Food Tradition

African Americans who lived under slavery's harsh hand were usually fed adequately by their white masters—but their meals often lacked meat. Many slaves, however, were allowed to supplement their diets by catching catfish from the creeks and rivers. A slave from Missouri remembered:

> I was too young to be put to work, and . . . spent my time . . . fishing. There was a creek nearby in which we caught plenty of fish. We made lines of hemp grown on the farm and hooks of bent pins. . . . But fish then were very plentiful. . . . We often brought home as much as five pounds of fish in a day.

Fried Catfish

Ingredients:

2 pounds thin catfish fillets, skinned
1½ teaspoons salt
¾ teaspoon black pepper
1 cup cornmeal
1 cup flour
1½ cups vegetable oil

Cooking utensils you'll need:
mixing bowl
measuring spoons
measuring cups
skillet

Directions:

Rinse fillets under the faucet and then dry with a paper towel. Mix together the salt, pepper, cornmeal, and flour. Heat the vegetable oil in heavy skillet over medium heat. *Dredge* the fillets in the seasoned cornmeal mixture. When the oil is hot (see tips on page 25), lay the fillets in the skillet a couple at a time. Cook about three minutes on each side, and then remove from the pan and drain on paper towels.

Tip:

Serve with lemon wedges.

Fried Pork Chops

Ingredients:

8 pork chops, ¼ to ½ inch thick
salt and black pepper to taste
1 cup flour
1 tablespoon paprika
1 cup vegetable oil

Cooking utensils you'll need:
measuring spoons
measuring cups
heavy plastic bag
skillet

Directions:

Rinse the meat and sprinkle salt and pepper on both sides. Put the flour and paprika in the plastic bag. Heat oil in the skillet. Shake pork chops in the bag until evenly coated with flour mixture. Shake off extra flour and place gently in the hot oil. Fry them 4 or 5 minutes on each side, until golden brown. Drain fat on paper towel and serve.

Tip:

Be very careful when cooking with hot oil not to burn yourself or stain your clothes. Keep the pan covered whenever possible.

African American Food History

"Soul food" uses a lot of pork. The roots of this food tradition lie back in slavery, when white plantation owners gave black workers the "throwaway" parts of a butchered pig—the feet, the hocks, the jowls, the ears, the skin, the fat . . . everything but the squeal! African American cooks learned to make good use of it all. They supplemented what was given them with meat they hunted—squirrel, rabbit, and possum.

As black women entered the plantation houses as cooks, they learned to cook with better cuts of pork. On their own tables, though, possum was still more common than pork chops. After working long hard hours, the evening meal was a time for families to feed both body and soul. Over the supper table, they retold their stories, they prayed and sang, and families and friends grew close. "Slave food" became known as "good times food," the ultimate comfort food.

African American Food History

Early African Americans ate a lot of greens—turnip greens, mustard greens, poke sallet, and collard greens. Many times these were wild plants or scraps thrown away from white kitchens—but they were good for you! Dark green leafy vegetables are packed with vitamins A and C, calcium and iron. The rich water in which the greens cooked was called "pot likka." It was good for dunking corn bread, and it helped children grow strong.

Collard Greens

This variety of cabbage doesn't form a head. It tastes a little like a cross between kale and cabbage.

Ingredients:

3 or 4 bunches of fresh collard greens (or you can use frozen)
2 cups of water
1 ham hock cut in small pieces
1 tablespoon sugar
1 teaspoon salt
½ teaspoon pepper

Cooking utensils you'll need:
measuring cups
measuring spoons
saucepan
sharp knife

Directions:

Place the ham hock in the water and boil for an hour. Meanwhile, wash the greens and remove stems; tear into bite-sized pieces. Add the greens and other ingredients to the water. Cover and cook over a low heat for about 2 hours, until the greens are tender.

Tips:

If you can't find a ham hock, you can use 1/4 pound of bacon cut into small pieces instead.

When buying collard greens fresh, look for crisp green leaves that haven't wilted or yellowed. It will last in a plastic bag in the refrigerator for 3 to 5 days.

Black-Eyed Peas

Ingredients:

1 pound dried black-eyed peas
4 cups water
1 medium onion, **diced**
½ teaspoon salt
¼ teaspoon pepper
1 cup cubed ham
¼ teaspoon red pepper (optional)

Cooking utensils you'll need:
measuring spoons
sharp knife
large cooking pot

Directions:

Wash the black-eyed peas. Soak overnight or bring to a boil in a large cooking pot. Add other ingredients and *simmer* on stovetop for 3 to 4 hours until peas are tender. Makes 6 to 8 servings.

Tip:

If you have a slow cooker, you can cook black-eyed peas all day instead of on the stovetop.

African American Food History

The black-eyed pea came from Africa to North America with the slaves. Tradition has it that if you eat black-eyed peas on New Year's Day, you'll have good luck through the year that follows.

African American Food History

Cornmeal was a staple for African American slaves. Most weekly rations included a peck of corn. Resourceful cooks used this in a variety of ways, but ground cornmeal was one of the most important. Cornmeal could be used for frying meat, as well as for baking into corn cakes, corn dodgers, hoe cakes, corn pone, cracklin' bread, and any number of other corn breads. Cracklin's (the crisp part left after the fat had been fried out of a pig's skin) were often used as flavoring.

Corn Bread

Preheat oven to 425 degrees Fahrenheit.

Ingredients:

¼ cup plus 2 tablespoons bacon grease (or butter or
vegetable shortening)
1 cup flour
4 teaspoons baking powder
½ teaspoon salt
2 tablespoons sugar
1 cup cornmeal
1 egg
1 cup milk

Cooking utensils you'll need:
measuring spoons
measuring cups
mixing bowl
small mixing bowl
8-inch square cake pan or round cast-iron skillet
mixing spoon

Directions:

Put 2 tablespoons bacon grease (or butter or shortening) into the pan or skillet. Set it on the warm oven so that the grease or butter melts, and the pan is evenly coated. Stir together dry ingredients in mixing bowl. Beat the egg in a separate bowl; then make a hollow in the center of the dry ingredients and pour in egg, milk, and the rest of the bacon grease or butter. Beat vigorously for about a minute. Bake for 20 to 25 minutes until golden brown.

Tip:

Corn bread is best served hot with butter. Some people like honey or jelly with it as well.

Corn Bread Stuffing

This stuffing can be used with chicken, turkey, or goose

Ingredients:

½ cup butter
1 large onion, chopped
1 cup chopped celery with the leaves included
4 cups crumbled cornbread (see page 37)
4 cups stale bread, cubed
1 **pinch** dried ground sage
1 teaspoon dried ground thyme
2 teaspoons poultry seasoning
1 teaspoon salt
¼ teaspoon pepper
1½ cups chicken **stock**

Cooking utensils you'll need:
measuring spoons
large frying pan
measuring cups
knife for cutting celery, onion, and bread

Directions:

Melt butter over low heat in frying pan. Add the onion and celery, and cook about 5 minutes until the onion looks transparent but not brown. Stir in corn bread and bread cubes, and continue cooking another 10 minutes until bread is golden brown. Add seasonings and stock. Makes enough to stuff a 15-pound turkey.

Tip:

If you don't have chicken stock, you can use canned chicken broth instead.

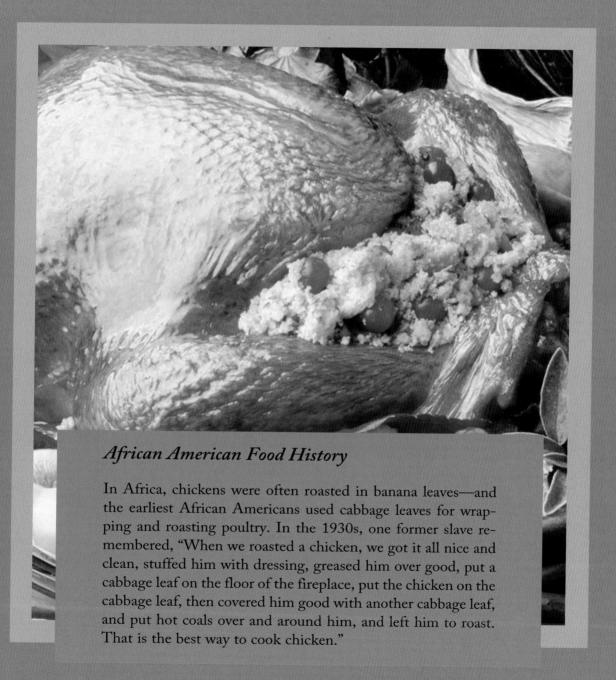

African American Food History

In Africa, chickens were often roasted in banana leaves—and the earliest African Americans used cabbage leaves for wrapping and roasting poultry. In the 1930s, one former slave remembered, "When we roasted a chicken, we got it all nice and clean, stuffed him with dressing, greased him over good, put a cabbage leaf on the floor of the fireplace, put the chicken on the cabbage leaf, then covered him good with another cabbage leaf, and put hot coals over and around him, and left him to roast. That is the best way to cook chicken."

African American Food History

Okra is a truly African food, brought to North America by the earliest African Americans. The word comes from the Niger-Congo languages spoken in West Africa. It is also called "lady's fingers," as well as "gombo," "gumbo," "okro," and "bamie." It comes from the same plant family as the marsh mallow (the source of the original marshmallow candy). The juice of the okra is used to thicken stews, and it gives its name to the "gumbo" that is so popular throughout much of the South.

Fried Okra

Okra is slimy and sticky. It's supposed to be that way!

Ingredients:

1 pound fresh okra
salt and pepper to taste
1 cup flour
1 cup cornmeal
shortening or bacon grease

Cooking utensils you'll need:
measuring cups
paring knife
skillet
plastic bag

Directions:

Wash the okra and cut off the ends; slice into ¼-inch pieces. Mix flour and cornmeal in a plastic bag with salt and pepper. Put the okra in the bag a little at a time and shake it around to coat it. When all of the okra is covered with the flour and cornmeal, fry it in ½ inch of grease or shortening in a skillet. Turn the okra over to lightly brown it on all sides (about 10 minutes). Drain on paper towel and serve hot.

Candied Yams

Preheat oven to 375 degrees Fahrenheit.

Ingredients:

4 medium-sized sweet potatoes
½ cup butter
1 tablespoon lemon juice
½ cup brown sugar, packed
½ cup water

Cooking utensils you'll need:
measuring cups
measuring spoons
large cooking pot
saucepan
2-quart baking dish

Directions:

Wash the sweet potatoes and then boil them whole (without peeling them) for 10 minutes. Meanwhile, make a syrup with the remaining ingredients and cook it for about 3 minutes over high heat, stirring constantly. When the potatoes are cool enough to handle, peel them and cut them into 1/2-inch thick slices. Put them in a buttered 2-quart baking dish, pour syrup over them, and bake, uncovered, for 30 to 40 minutes until golden brown. *Baste* a couple of times during baking.

Tip:

You can add nuts, nutmeg, cinnamon, or marshmallows to this dish to make it still sweeter and richer.

African American Food History

Sweet potatoes are one of the oldest vegetables known to human beings. They have been consumed since prehistoric times (as evidenced by
sweet potato relics that have been discovered in Peruvian caves dating
back 10,000 years). Christopher Columbus brought sweet potatoes to
Europe after his first voyage in 1492. By the 16th century, sweet potatoes began to be cultivated in what is now the southern United States.

Although the words *yam* and *sweet potato* are often used interchange-
ably, true yams are an African plant that is seldom grown in the United
States. There are over 150 species of yams grown throughout the
world—and the largest can grow as big as 7½ feet long, weighing as
much as 120 pounds!

Sweet Potato Fries

Ingredients:

4 sweet potatoes
pinch of salt
water
3 cups vegetable oil

Cooking utensils you'll need:
paring knife
measuring cups
saucepan
colander
large cooking pot

Directions:

Wash and scrub sweet potatoes, and then *parboil* them for 10 minutes in enough salted water to cover them. Drain off water. As soon as they are cool enough for you to handle, peel them and cut into thin strips the size of ordinary French fries. Meanwhile, heat the vegetable oil over high heat. The oil is hot enough when a potato bubbles when it is dropped into the oil. Fry potatoes for 3 minutes or until golden brown. Drain on paper towel. Serve hot.

Tips:

Always be very careful when using hot oil not to start a fire or burn yourself.

Sweet potato fries are good sprinkled with salt—or with brown sugar and nutmeg.

African American Food History

When African Americans arrived in North America, sweet potatoes were much like the yams they knew back in their own land. White people often used the orange potatoes for livestock feed, reserving the white potatoes for their own tables—but African Americans knew the value of these sweet orange tubers. Sweet potatoes are far richer in vitamins and fiber than white potatoes, and better for you too.

Rice and Beans

Ingredients:

2 cups dried pinto beans
6 cups water
1 small onion, chopped
8 ounces diced ham
salt and pepper to taste
1 cup rice

Cooking utensils you'll need:
measuring cups
sharp knife
saucepan
large pot

Directions:

Wash the beans, and then bring to a boil in a large pot with 4 cups water, onion, and ham. Lower the heat and simmer until the beans are tender, about 3 hours. Put rice in a saucepan with 2 cups water and bring to a boil over high heat. Lower heat and *simmer* until all the water is absorbed, about 20 minutes. Mix rice with beans and serve.

African American Food Tradition

According to Sheila Ferguson, author of *Soul Food*:

> In soul food, beans and rice always go together. They
> say there's a nutritional reason for this, but I reckon on
> another one. Simmered slow and easy the soul food
> way . . . , your beans come out with a sumptuously
> thick and soulful gravy that can make a big man weep.
> And what better to pick up the flavor and make sure it
> reaches your tastebuds than a generous bed of rice?

Beans and rice have probably been cooked and eaten together
since prehistoric times. Africans still cook the same dish that is a
favorite of their American relatives. Cooking the beans and rice
in the same pot (after giving the beans a head start) is likely the
original cooking method.

African American Food Tradition

During the early twentieth century, Sunday dinners became a common time for African American families to get together. Adult sons and daughters would travel far for a good home-cooked meal. Aunts, mothers, grandmothers, and daughters would gather in the kitchen and cook up a storm, and then the family would sit down around a table heavy with watermelon, ribs, sweet potatoes, greens, fried chicken—and potato salad.

Today, the aroma of "soul food" still fills homes on Sunday afternoons. As it filters down the street, the neighbors know that a good meal is in the making. Some of them may find an excuse to drop by. . . .

Potato Salad

Ingredients:

3 cup cooked potatoes, cubed
2 hard–boiled eggs, chopped
½ cup chopped celery
½ cup **diced** onions
½ teaspoon salt
1 teaspoon vinegar
½ teaspoon pepper
1 cup mayonnaise
1 teaspoon mustard

Cooking utensils you'll need:
large mixing bowl
measuring cups
measuring spoons

Directions:

Mix ingredients together. Cover and refrigerate at least 2 hours.

Tip:

Some people like to add ½ cup sweet pickle relish or ¼ teaspoon celery seed to potato salad.

Peanut Soup

Ingredients:

½ cup finely chopped onion
2 tablespoons vegetable oil
¾ cup creamy peanut butter
3 cups chicken broth
salt and pepper to taste

Cooking utensils you'll need:
measuring cups
measuring spoons
large saucepan

Directions:

Cook onion in oil until soft and golden brown. Blend in peanut butter. Add chicken broth, stirring constantly until mixture is smooth. Bring to a boil, then lower heat, and *simmer* 10 minutes. Makes 4 to 6 servings.

African American Food History

When Africans were brought to North America as slaves, peanuts came with them. The first African Americans planted peanuts throughout the southern United States. (The word goober comes from nguba, the Congo name for peanuts.) In the 1700s, peanuts, then called groundnuts or ground peas, were regarded as an excellent food for pigs. Until the twentieth century, peanuts were not grown much, partly because they were regarded as food for the poor, and partly because growing and harvesting them was a slow and difficult process until labor-saving equipment was invented around the turn of the century. Dr. George Washington Carver, the son of Missouri slaves, developed more than 300 products from peanuts, adding to their popularity.

Sweet Potato Pie

Preheat oven to 350 degrees Fahrenheit.

Ingredients:

3 cups mashed sweet potatoes
3 eggs
1 cup sugar
¾ teaspoon salt
¾ teaspoon nutmeg
1½ teaspoon cinnamon
½ teaspoon allspice
1 cup heavy cream
1 unbaked 10-inch piecrust

Cooking utensils you'll need:
measuring cups
measuring spoons
mixing bowl
10-inch pie plate

Directions:

Beat all the ingredients together. Pour into unbaked piecrust. Bake for 1 hour, until center of the pie is firm. (A knife or toothpick inserted in the center will come out clean.) Cool and serve with whipped cream.

Tip:

You can buy ready-made piecrust. Or you can make your own from 1½ cups flour, ½ teaspoon salt, ½ cup shortening, 3 tablespoons cold water. Roll out the dough until it's about ⅛ thick. If you roll it between two sheets of wax paper, you can easily peel off one sheet, put the crust dough-side down in a pie plate, and then peel off the other sheet of wax paper.

African American Food Tradition

African Americans love sweet things, and their desserts are rich and wonderful. Author Sheila Ferguson refers to soul food as "fun-loving, toe-tapping, belly-busting . . . cuisine." But, she says, it has a more serious side too.

> This style of cooking was carved out of the deep South by the black slaves, in part for their white masters and in part for their own survival in the slave quarters. As such, it is like the blues or jazz, an inextricable part of the African-Americans' struggle to survive and express themselves. In this sense it is *true* American cuisine, because it wasn't imported into America by immigrants like so many other ethnic offerings. It is the cuisine of the American dream, if you like. Because what can't be cured must be endured.

Try sweet potato pie. You may find its sweetness gives strength for enduring the hardships of life!

African American Food History

Pecan trees were growing wild in North America when the first humans crossed the Bering Strait from Asia before 8,000 B.C.E. Those first inhabitants were hunter-gatherers and collected the nuts in autumn for the long cold winters.

Native Americans relied on pecans as an important food staple, and the early settlers, both white and black, learned survival lessons from the Indians. American Indians taught them how to gather and use the nuts for sustenance.

Pecans grew wild throughout the south, but in the mid 1800s, a Louisiana slave named Antoine developed a method to improve the quality of the wild pecan and increased the trees' productivity. Antoine created the pecan variety called "Centennial" at the Oak Alley Plantation. About 500 modern-day varieties of cultivated pecan trees originated from Centennial.

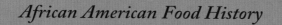

Pecan Pie

Preheat oven to 325 degrees Fahrenheit.

Ingredients:

¼ cup softened butter
½ cup brown sugar, packed
½ cup white sugar
3 eggs
½ cup corn syrup
2 teaspoons vanilla
½ teaspoon salt
1 cup coarsely ground pecans
½ cup whole pecan halves
1 ready-made 9-inch piecrust

Cooking utensils you'll need:
measuring cups
measuring spoons
mixing bowl
9-inch pie plate

Directions:

Cream butter and sugars, and then blend in eggs. Stir in remaining ingredients except the whole pecan halves. Pour into the unbaked piecrust and arrange pecan halves on top to look pretty. Bake for 1 hour. Serve warm with ice cream or whipped cream.

Tip:

See page 53 if you want to make your own crust.

African American Food Tradition

Peaches are one of the fruits that are often eaten for Kwanzaa, the seven-day celebration that was created by Dr. Maulana Karenga to promote unity and pride among African Americans. Kwanzaa is a spiritual and joyous celebration developed to showcase the growth and development of the African American community.

The word "kwanza" comes from a Swahili phrase that means "the first fruits." An extra "a" was added to the word to make it seven letters to correspond with the length of the holiday and to the seven principles, called the Nguzo Saba. Each day of the holiday represents one principle.

Peach Cobbler

Preheat oven to 350 degrees Fahrenheit.

Ingredients:

1 stick of melted butter
2 cups biscuit mix (Bisquick® is one example)
2 cups milk
2 cups sugar
1 large can of peaches

Cooking utensils you'll need:
measuring cups
mixing bowl
13x9-inch pan

Directions:

Put melted butter in the pan. Mix biscuit mix, sugar, and milk together, and pour into pan. Cut peaches into pieces and add to flour mixture. Cover with foil and bake for 15 minutes. Then uncover and bake another 15 minutes. Serve warm with ice cream.

Tip:

You can use 4 fresh peaches instead of canned peaches. Peel the fruit and cut in slices, removing the pit.

Sesame Seed Cookies

These traditional African American cookies are also called Benne Cakes. (Benne is the West African word for sesame seed.)

Ingredients:

1 cup packed brown sugar
¼ cup butter or margarine, softened
1 egg
½ teaspoon vanilla
1 teaspoon freshly squeezed lemon juice
½ cup flour
½ teaspoon baking powder
¼ teaspoon salt
1 cup toasted sesame seeds

Cooking utensils you'll need:
measuring cups
measuring spoons
mixing bowl
cookie sheet

Directions:

Mix together the sugar and butter, and beat until they are creamy. Stir in the egg, vanilla, and lemon juice. Add flour, baking powder, salt, and sesame seeds. Drop by rounded teaspoons onto a greased cookie sheet 2 inches apart. Bake for 15 minutes or until the edges are browned.

African American Food Tradition

Sesame seed cookies are a traditional food symbolizing good luck at Kwanzaa. Each day of the Kwanzaa holiday, which is celebrated from December 26 until January 1st, represents one of the seven principles:

1. **umoja**: unity, importance of togetherness for the family and the community.
2. **kujichagulia**: self-determination, defining common interests and making decisions that are in the best interest of family and community.
3. **ujima**: collective work and responsibility, reminder of the obligation to the past, present, and future, and the importance of roles that are played in the community, society, and world.
4. **ujamma**: cooperative economics, reminder of the collective economic strength and encouragement to meet common needs through mutual support.
5. **nia**: purpose, looking within to set personal goals that will be beneficial to the community.
6. **kuumba**: creativity, using creative energies to build and maintain a strong and vibrant community.
7. **imani**: faith, focuses on honoring the best of traditions, drawing upon the best in self, the need to strive for a higher level of life for humankind, by affirming self-worth and confidence in the ability to succeed and triumph in righteous struggle.

African American Food Traditions

The following items are needed for a Kwanzaa celebration:

MKEKA (m-kay-cah): a straw mat (place mat), which is very important because all of the other items are placed upon it.

KINARA (kee-nah-rah): a candleholder that holds seven candles to reflect the seven principles that are the foundation of Kwanzaa.

MSHUMAA (mee-shoo-maah): seven candles to represent the Seven Principles, one black, three red, and three green.

MAZAO (mah-ZAH-oh): the Crops, the fruits and vegetables that are the result of the harvest. Bananas, apples, mangoes, peaches, plantains, oranges, or whatever might be the family favorites. The Mazao are placed on the Mkeka and are shared and eaten to honor the work of the people it took to grow them.

MUHINDI (moo-heen-dee): ears of corn to represent the children (and future) of the family. One suke (ear) of corn is placed on the Mkeka for each child in the family. If there are no children in the family one suke is still placed on the Mkeka to symbolize the children of the community.

KIKOMBE CHA UMOJA (kee-coam-bay chah-oo-moe-jah): the unity cup; when filled with water, juice, or wine, a little bit is poured out as a reminder of the ancestors. Each member of the immediate family or extended family drinks from the cup in a gesture of honor, praise, collective work, and commitment to continue the struggle begun by their ancestors.

ZAWADI (sah-wah-dee): gifts that are enriching and will bless and help the community, gifts given to children that will make them better people. The gifts should always include a book, video, or other educational item that will educate and inform the child. There should also be a gift known as a "heritage symbol," something to remind the child of glory of the past and promise of the future.

Apple Pie

Preheat oven to 425 degrees Fahrenheit.

Ingredients:

2 ready-made piecrusts
8–10 apples
1 teaspoon lemon juice
1 cup sugar
½ cup flour
1 teaspoon cinnamon
¼ teaspoon nutmeg
¼ teaspoon salt
2 tablespoons butter or margarine

Cooking utensils you'll need:
measuring cups
measuring spoons
mixing bowl
9-inch pie plate
sharp knife
peeler

Directions:

Press one piecrust into a pie plate. Peel and core apples and cut into thin slices. Drop them into lemon juice. (It will keep the apples from turning brown.) Add the sugar, flour, cinnamon, nutmeg, and salt, and *toss* the apples until they're evenly coated. Put the apple mixture into the piecrust and dot with butter. Place the remaining piecrust on top. Seal the edges of the two crusts, and cut a hole in the center to allow steam to escape. Bake for 50 minutes until the crust is evenly browned.

Tip:

If the edges of the crust look like they're turning brown faster than the middle is baking, you can reduce the oven to 350. You can also press narrow strips of aluminum foil around the edge of the pie to prevent the edges from burning.

Further Reading

Ferguson, Sheila. *Soul Food: Classic Cuisine from the Deep South.* New York: Grove Press, 1999.

National Council of Negro Women. *The Black Family Reunion Cookbook: Recipes and Food Memories from the National Council of Negro Women, Inc.* New York: Fireside, 1993.

Sanna, Ellyn. *Food Folklore.* Philadelphia, Penn.: Mason Crest Publishers, 2003.

White, Joyce. *Brown Sugar: Soul Food Desserts from Family and Friends.* New York: HarperCollins, 2003.

———. *Soul Food: Recipes and Reflections from African–American Churches.* New York: HarperCollins, 1998.

Woods, Sylvia. *Sylvia's Family Soul Food Cookbook: From Hemingway, South Carolina, to Harlem.* New York: Morrow, 1999.

For More Information

African American Culture
www.straightblack.com/African/American/Culture/

Kwanzaa
www.kidsdomain.com/holiday/kwanzaa/index.html
members.cox.net/in2vabeach/kwanzaa4kids/welcome.htm

Kwanzaa Recipes
www.www.foodnetwork.com/food/et_hd_kwanzaa/0,1972,FOOD_9838,00.html

Soul Food
www.soulfoodcookbook.com
chitterlings.com
www.thegutsygourmet.net/soul.html

Index

African American cooking techniques 8, 24, 39
American Indians 55
Apple Pie 65

Barbecue Pork Sandwich 26–27
Barbecue Sauce 21–22
beans and rice 47
Black-Eyed Peas 34

Candied Yams 42
catfish 28
Collard Greens 33
cooking glossary 16–17
Corn Bread 37
cornmeal 36

European explorers 8

Ferguson, Sheila 47, 54
Fried Catfish 29
Fried Chicken 25
Fried Okra 41
Fried Pork Chops 30

greens 32

Kwanzaa 58, 62–63

metric conversion table 14

okra 40

Peach Cobbler 59
peaches 58
Peanut Soup 50
peanuts 50
Pecan Pie 56
pecans 55
Potato Salad 49
pork 31

rent parties 23
Rice and Beans 46

safety tips 12–13
seasoning 27
Sesame Seed Cookies 60
slavery 8, 23, 24, 28, 31, 34, 36, 50

soul food 8, 23, 31, 47, 54
Sunday dinners 48
Sweet Potato Fries 45
Sweet Potato Pie 53
sweet potatoes 43, 45

utensils 15

yams 43, 45

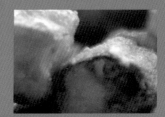

Author:

Ellyn Sanna is the author of *101 Easy Supper Recipes for Busy Moms* from Promise Press, and several recipe gift books from Barbour Publishing, including *Feast*, *An Invitation to Tea*, and the books in the "Christmas at Home" series. A former middle school teacher and the mother of three children ages eleven through sixteen, she has experience addressing both the learning needs and the food tastes of young cooks. Ellyn Sanna has also authored and edited numerous educational titles.

Food Preparer:

Theo's Southern Style Cuisine is owned and operated by the Felton family, who delight in providing Southern hospitality in a down-home atmosphere. Their meals are prepared from recipes passed down through the generations since the Antebellum period in southern Georgia. The Feltons migrated north in 1956 and have provided quality meals and catering services for over thirty years in southern New York and northeastern Pennsylvania.

Consultant:

The Culinary Institute of America is considered the world's premier culinary college. It is a private, not-for-profit learning institution, dedicated to providing the world's best culinary education. Its campuses in New York and California provide learning environments that focus on excellence, leadership, professionalism, ethics, and respect for diversity. The institute embodies a passion for food with first-class cooking expertise.

Recipe Contributor:

Rosa Waters has been cooking soul food since she was a child. Her family recipes are wonderful representatives of the African American food heritage.

NATURE'S
CHILDREN

BLUE WHALES

by Ruth Bjorklund

Children's Press®

An Imprint of Scholastic Inc.
New York Toronto London Auckland Sydney
Mexico City New Delhi Hong Kong
Danbury, Connecticut

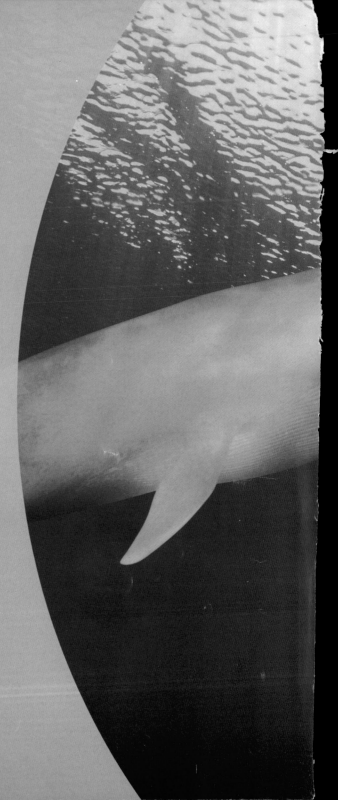

Content Consultant
Dr. Stephen S. Ditchkoff
Professor of Wildlife Sciences
Auburn University
Auburn, Alabama

Photographs © 2014: age fotostock: 15 (John Hyde), 16 (Michael
S. Nolan); AP Images: 28 (Museo Paleontologico de Caldera),
31 (North Wind Picture Archives); Bob Italiano: 44-45 map; Getty
Images/Popperfoto: 32; Landov/Amos Nachoun/Bancroft Media:
11; Minden Picture: cover, 20 (Flip Nicklin), 24 (Hiroya Minakuch),
23 (Martin Camm); Science Source/Francois Gohier: 5 top inset, 8;
Shutterstock, Inc./Rich Carey: 2-3 background, 44-45 background;
Superstock, Inc.: 19 (BlueGreen Pictures), 1, 7, 46 (Gohier/
VWPics), 2-3 foreground, 5 bottom inset, 40 (Mark Conlin VWPics),
4, 5 background, 12, 27, 36, 39 (Minden Pictures); The Granger
Collection: 35.

Library of Congress Cataloging-in-Publication Data
Bjorklund, Ruth.
 Blue whales / by Ruth Bjorklund.
 p. cm.—(Nature's children)
 Summary: "This book details the life and habits of blue whales." —
Provided by publisher.
 Audience: 9–12.
 Audience: Grades 4 to 6.
 Includes bibliographical references and index.
 ISBN 978-0-531-23355-9 (lib. bdg.) — ISBN 978-0-531-25153-9
(pbk.)
 1. Blue whale—Juvenile literature. 2. Blue whale—Conservation—
Juvenile literature. I. Title. II. Series: Nature's children (New York, N.Y.)
 QL737.C424B56 2013
 599.5'248—dc23   2013000086

Printed in China 62
SCHOLASTIC, CHILDREN'S PRESS, and associated logos are
trademarks and/or registered trademarks of Scholastic Inc.

1 2 3 4 5 6 7 8 9 10 R 23 22 21 20 19 18 17 16 15 14

Blue Whales

Class	Mammalia
Order	Cetacea
Family	Balaenopteridae
Genus	*Balaenoptera*
Species	*Balaenoptera musculus*
World distribution	Worldwide, mainly in the North Atlantic Ocean, North Pacific Ocean, and Southern Hemisphere; most blue whales migrate seasonally from polar oceans to warmer oceans and seas
Habitats	Polar and subpolar ocean regions; tropical and subtropical oceans and seas
Distinctive physical characteristics	The largest animals ever known to have existed; bluish-gray; a streamlined, torpedo shape; flat head; baleen plates; throat grooves; small dorsal fin; strong flippers; wide tail flukes
Habits	Often solitary; sometimes live in small groups; most feed in cold oceans in summer and warmer waters in winter
Diet	Krill

BLUE WHALES

Contents

CHAPTER 1
6 Mysterious and Mighty

CHAPTER 2
13 Creatures of the Deep

CHAPTER 3
21 Life at Sea

CHAPTER 4
29 A Whale's Tale

CHAPTER 5
34 Today and Tomorrow

42 Words to Know

44 Habitat Map

46 Find Out More

47 Index

48 About the Author

Mysterious and Mighty

With a splash, a boom, and a giant blast of spray, a blue whale exhales and dives below the surface of the ocean. This massive creature is the longest and heaviest animal on Earth and probably the largest that has ever lived. On average, it weighs 200,000 to 300,000 pounds (90,719 to 136,078 kilograms) and reaches lengths of 70 to 90 feet (21 to 27 meters). A blue whale can be as long as three school buses and 25 times larger than the extinct *Tyrannosaurus rex*.

Blue whales are bluish gray. Their bodies are sleek and smooth. They have flat heads, pectoral flippers, and small dorsal fins. There are two pads called flukes at the end of a blue whale's tail. A blue whale has two nostrils called blowholes on the top of its head. Instead of teeth, it has baleen plates that filter food.

The immense blue whale would have dwarfed even the largest dinosaurs.

Mammals at Sea

Blue whales are mammals. Like all mammals, they breathe oxygen into their lungs. Baby whales grow inside the mother's bodies, and infants drink their mothers' milk. They also have ears, ribs, vertebrae, and thin patches of hair.

Blue whales rise to the water's surface to breathe. They breathe in and out several times, spouting towers of used air, mucus, and sea spray from their blowholes. The "blow" of the blue whale is the tallest, strongest, and loudest of all whales, rising 30 feet (9 m) or more. With their lungs full of air, blue whales can swim underwater for 10 to 20 minutes at a time, and sometimes longer.

Blue whales must swim constantly to breathe. They drown if they stop moving. As a result, they do not sleep. Instead, they rest one-half of their brain at a time and let the other half stay awake.

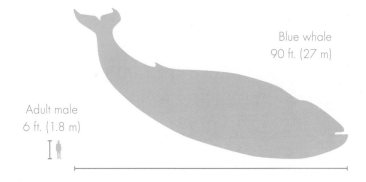

Blue whale
90 ft. (27 m)

Adult male
6 ft. (1.8 m)

A huge jet of water and air erupts every time a blue whale breathes.

From Sea to Sea

There are three main groups of blue whales, organized by where they live: the North Atlantic Ocean, the North Pacific Ocean, and the Southern Hemisphere. Most blue whales spend the summer feeding in the nutrient-rich waters of the earth's northern and southern oceans. Come fall, the whales migrate thousands of miles to warm waters near the equator.

The seasons in the Northern Hemisphere are the opposite of those in the Southern Hemisphere, so the groups of whales never meet. The northern blue whales migrate south to the equator in September, and the southern blue whales migrate north to the equator in April. There are also some blue whales living in the Pacific Ocean near Costa Rica and in the Indian Ocean near Sri Lanka that do not migrate. The waters in these areas stay warm enough for these whales to live there all year.

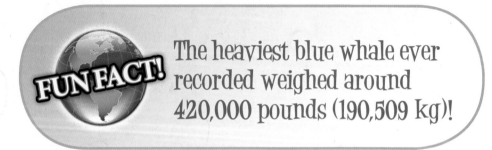

FUN FACT! The heaviest blue whale ever recorded weighed around 420,000 pounds (190,509 kg)!

Divers have closely observed the blue whales that live near Sri Lanka.

CHAPTER 2

Creatures of the Deep

Blue whales are built to survive in oceans around the world. Their streamlined, torpedo-shaped bodies glide easily through water. Their heads are flat. Their skin is smooth, oily, rubbery, and flexible. While the whales swim, small folds form in their skin to help water slide quickly across their bodies.

Blue whales swim and dive by moving their tails and flukes in powerful up and down strokes. They use their flippers mainly for steering and stopping. Adult blue whales barely rise above the water when they surface for air. But sometimes they lift their flukes, which are usually 10 to 13 feet (3 to 4 m) long, and slap them loudly on the water before they dive. This is called lobtailing.

A blue whale can move a tremendous amount of water with a simple flick of its tail fluke.

Speed and Danger

Compared to most other whales, blue whales are fast swimmers. They usually swim at speeds of around 13 miles (21 kilometers) per hour. When they are in pain or in danger, however, they can reach speeds of 20 to 30 miles (32 to 48 km) per hour. Blue whales usually swim at depths of around 300 feet (91 m), but they can dive to 1,600 feet (488 m) or more if they are threatened.

Adult blue whales do not have predators in the natural world. They are too large and too fast to be caught. But sometimes a pod of orca whales will attack a young blue whale. The orcas, also called killer whales, will surround and harass a young blue whale until it is too tired to escape.

At an average length of around 26 feet (8 m), orcas are only a fraction of a blue whale's size, but they pose a serious threat to blue whales that aren't fully grown.

Conserving Energy

Like all mammals, blue whales are warm-blooded. They must keep their body temperature near 98 degrees Fahrenheit (37 degrees Celsius). Land mammals have many ways to keep warm, such as sleeping in the sun or curling up in nests. But blue whales live in water that can be as cold as 28°F (–2°C). They stay warm by storing huge amounts of fat under their skin. This fat is called blubber.

Blue whales are so large and travel so far that they need a great deal of energy to survive. They use 90 percent of the oxygen they breathe into their lungs. An average human, on the other hand, uses only about 15 percent of the oxygen in each breath. A blue whale's heart weighs between 1,000 and 2,000 pounds (454 and 907 kg) and pumps more than 14,000 pounds (6,350 kg) of blood through the whale's body to keep it healthy and warm.

FUN FACT! A blue whale's heart is the size of a small car.

Blue whales generally spend summers in the freezing cold waters near the North and South Poles.

Sensing the Seas

Blue whales can see, hear, and feel. They open their eyes wide underwater to absorb as much light as possible. In daylight above water, they narrow their eyes into slits because the light is bright.

Hearing is a blue whale's strongest sense. On the outside, its ears are small holes filled with wax. Sound waves travel through water, vibrate through the wax, and reach the whale's inner ears in the skull. Because of the wax, blue whales are nearly deaf above the water's surface, but a blue whale can hear another blue whale more than 1,000 miles (1,609 km) away when it is underwater!

A blue whale's sense of touch is especially strong around its blowholes. When the whale comes up for air, it cannot see if its blowholes are above water. Instead, it relies on its sense of touch. The whale knows that it is safe to breathe when it feels open air around its blowhole. Scientists believe that blue whales have very little, if any, sense of smell or taste.

A blue whale's eyes are very small compared to the size of its head.

CHAPTER 3

Life at Sea

Amazingly, the largest animal on Earth survives by eating one of the planet's tiniest creatures. A blue whale's diet is made up almost entirely of a single food called krill. Krill is a tiny, shrimplike zooplankton that is plentiful in the waters of the North Pacific, North Atlantic, and Antarctic Oceans.

Blue whales feed six to eight months of the year, eating as much as 8,500 to 13,000 pounds (3,856 to 5,897 kg) of krill every day. During the feeding season, blue whales eat more than their daily need and save the extra energy as blubber. Blue whales eat very little once they begin their migration to warm water. For four to six months, they mainly use the energy stored in their blubber. However, they will temporarily stop migrating to feed if they find an especially good food source along the way.

Krill are tiny animals just 2.5 inches (6.35 cm) long that look like shrimp.

How They Eat

Blue whales have fringed plates in their mouths that are used to filter food. The plates are made of baleen, a substance containing a protein called keratin. This is the same material found in human hair and fingernails. The baleen grows in plates from the whales' upper jaws. A blue whale has 250 to 400 plates on each side of its mouth. The outside of the baleen is smooth, but the inside strands of baleen are frayed and matted together.

A blue whale has between 60 and 90 grooves along its throat from the lower jaw to the belly. When blue whales eat, they lunge upward through a school of krill and gulp in krill and seawater. The grooves unfold to make the whale's mouth several times bigger. An adult blue whale can hold as much as 15,000 pounds (6,804 kg) of seawater and krill in its mouth at one time.

Blue whales use their tongues to push the water and krill through their baleen plates. The water is forced out, and the krill is snagged by the rough inside strands of baleen. Then the whales use their tongues to scrape the krill from the baleen so they can swallow it.

A blue whale's tongue weighs more than an average elephant.

Baby Blues

Blue whales breed and raise their young in warm waters. A mother blue whale gives birth to a baby whale, called a calf, about once every two to three years. The gestation period of a blue whale is 11 to 12 months. When a baby blue whale is born, its mother nudges it to the surface for its first breath. Blue whale calves are able to swim as soon as they are born.

A newborn calf weighs 4,400 to 5,500 pounds (1,996 to 2,495 kg) and is 23 to 26 feet (7 to 8 m) long. That means that even a baby blue whale is larger than an average car! The calf drinks about 90 gallons (341 liters) of its mother's milk each day. A blue whale calf is one of the fastest-growing animals on Earth. During the first year of its life, it can grow as much as 200 pounds (91 kg) per day! After spending the winter in warm water near the equator, the young whale is ready to migrate to the summer feeding areas with its mother.

Young blue whales rarely stray far from their mother's side.

Going Solo

Blue whales do not live in large pods. Sometimes blue whales travel in small groups of two to four, but many migrate alone. Calves migrate with their mothers. They separate once they reach their feeding grounds. Although blue whales feed mostly alone, sometimes a group of blue whales will work as a team to round up schools of krill.

Many scientists believe that blue whales communicate with one another over long distances. Male blue whales make a deep humming sound that can travel hundreds of miles through the water. Scientists who study the sounds wonder if blue whales could be using these sounds to look for **mates** or to tell each other about food sources. They also wonder if blue whales make sounds to guide one another as they migrate.

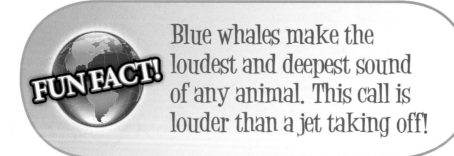

FUN FACT!

Blue whales make the loudest and deepest sound of any animal. This call is louder than a jet taking off!

On rare occasions, blue whales group together to feed on krill.

CHAPTER 4

A Whale's Tale

The ancestors of blue whales were land-dwelling mammals. Deer, cattle, and hippopotamuses are also related to these extinct animals. Fossil skeletons dating back 50 million years show that whale ancestors had four legs, teeth, and a doglike snout. Over 35 million years, they slowly changed. Their hind legs disappeared, and their front legs became flippers. They developed baleen plates instead of teeth. Their nostrils shifted and turned into blowholes. Around 15 million years ago, the ancestors of today's blue whales became marine mammals.

Today's whales belong to the order of animals called Cetacea. Cetacea is divided into two suborders: toothed whales and baleen whales. The three groups of baleen whales are right whales, gray whales, and rorquals. Rorquals have grooved throats and a pair of blowholes. The blue whale is the largest rorqual, and the sei whale is the fastest. Other rorquals include the Bryde's whale, fin whale, humpback whale, and minke whale.

Scientists must unearth fossils very carefully to avoid damaging them.

Whaling

In the 17th century, hunting whales, or whaling, started to become common. By the 19th century, it was a major industry. People wanted whale blubber for lamp oil. They also used it to grease machinery and make cooking oil, soap, and perfumes. Baleen was used to make everyday items such as umbrellas and hairbrushes. To meet this demand, North American, European, and Asian whalers hunted whales aboard large sailing ships. They speared whales with harpoons, cut them open, cut out the blubber, and boiled the blubber into oil.

At first, blue whales were too hard to catch. They were strong and quick, and swam far from land. But in the mid-1800s, whaling changed. New whaling ships were faster and could go much farther. In 1868, an exploding harpoon was invented. This weapon killed blue whales and other large whales quickly, before they could escape.

During the 19th century, huge whaling ships traveled the world's oceans in search of highly valuable whale blubber.

A Dwindling Population

By the beginning of the 20th century, whale oil was no longer in demand for lighting. But it was still used to make soap and margarine. An Antarctic explorer named Captain Carl Larsen discovered tens of thousands of blue whales living near Antarctica. He established a whaling port on a remote island called South Georgia Island.

In 1914, World War I was raging in Europe. It was discovered that whale oil could be used to make bombs. Each blue whale could supply 30,000 to 40,000 pounds (13,608 to 18,144 kg) of oil. Between 1914 and 1915, Larsen's whaling fleet killed thousands of blue whales. Later, in 1930 and 1931, almost 30,000 blue whales were killed in Antarctica, the largest amount ever in a single whaling season. Before Captain Larsen arrived, there were 150,000 to 200,000 blue whales in the Southern Hemisphere. After 70 years of whaling, there were fewer than 2,000.

The Norwegian explorer Carl Larsen was one of the leading whalers of the 20th century.

CHAPTER 5

Today and Tomorrow

For millions of years, blue whales swam peacefully throughout the world's oceans. But in the last century, 200,000 to 250,000 blue whales were killed. Now blue whales are on the international list of endangered species.

In 1931, 22 countries signed an agreement to keep track of whale populations. That year, 43,000 whales of all species were killed. In 1946, the International Whaling Commission (IWC) was set up to control whale hunting around the world. The IWC set limits on whale hunting. The limits were measured in Blue Whale Units (BWU). A BWU is the amount of oil found in one blue whale. One BWU equaled one blue whale, two fin whales, two and a half humpback whales, or six sei whales. Whalers realized it was easier to catch one blue whale than to catch more than one of the other whales. They killed so many blue whales that the species almost became extinct. In 1966, the IWC banned all hunting of blue whales.

Before laws were passed in the 1930s and 1940s, whalers were allowed to kill as many whales as they wanted.

Modern Threats

Although there are laws protecting blue whales today, they still face many dangers. The two biggest threats to their safety are collisions with large, fast-moving ships and getting tangled in fishing gear.

They are also threatened by other serious problems, such as water pollution and climate change. Oil spills and garbage thrown from boats harm the whales' habitat. Scientists have found harmful chemicals in the blubber of blue whales. They also report that climate change from air pollution is making the oceans warmer. The warmer water increases the growth of parasites and germs, which can make the whales sick. Warm water also reduces the supply of krill, which only thrive in cool water. Noise pollution is another problem. Noise from underwater testing and big ships interferes with the blue whales' ability to hear.

In the western Northern Atlantic Ocean, at least 9 percent of the blue whale population have injuries or scars from shipping vessels.

Coasting Along

Whale experts believe there were between 150,000 to 200,000 blue whales before whaling. Now there are between 5,000 to 12,000 left in the world. The healthiest group lives in the North Pacific and migrates to the coasts of Costa Rica, Mexico, and California. Recently, whale watchers have seen as many as 3,000 blue whales feeding on krill along the California coast. The U.S. government has ordered all large ships to reduce their speed in this area to avoid hitting the whales.

Today, scientists are using modern technologies to study blue whales. They are tagging blue whales and tracking their migrations by satellite. In the United States, they are using the navy's underwater listening devices to locate the whales. They have been able to hear blue whales humming from 1,500 miles (2,414 km) away.

Scientists use special tools to attach tracking devices to blue whales.

40

Time Will Tell

Blue whales live for 70 to 90 years. Some blue whales alive today may have barely escaped Captain Larsen's harpoon gun when they were younger. Blue whales take a long time to reproduce. Their habitats are threatened. It will take decades to see if they will recover from their decreased numbers.

Around the world, people are looking for ways to keep the blue whale from extinction. There are important laws, such as the U.S. Marine Mammal Protection Act and the Antarctic Conservation Act, that provide protection to whales and other endangered species. There are also conservation groups that teach people about ways to save threatened animals such as blue whales. Blue whales depend on clean, cold water to thrive. Helping to prevent air and water pollution and conserving energy are important steps everyone can take to protect and save the mighty blue whales.

Educating people about the difficulties blue whales face will help ensure that these gigantic sea mammals survive for many years to come.

Words to Know

ancestors (AN-ses-turz) — ancient animal species that are related to modern species

baleen (BAY-leen) — fringed plates made of keratin that hang from the upper jaw of a baleen whale

climate (KLYE-mit) — the weather typical of a place over a long period of time

conservation (kahn-sur-VAY-shuhn) — the protection of valuable things, especially forests, wildlife, natural resources, or artistic or historic objects

dorsal (DOR-suhl) — relating to the upper side or back of an animal

endangered (en-DAYN-jurd) — at risk of becoming extinct, usually because of human activity

equator (i-KWAY-tur) — an imaginary line around the middle of the earth that is an equal distance from the North and South Poles

extinct (ik-STINGKT) — no longer found alive; known about only through fossils or history

flukes (FLOOKS) — parts of the tail of a sea creature such as a whale or dolphin

fossil (FAH-suhl) — a bone, shell, or other trace of an animal or plant from long ago, preserved as rock

gestation (jes-TAY-shun) — the period of time that unborn young are within the mother

habitat (HAB-uh-tat) — the place where an animal or a plant naturally lives

mammals (MAM-uhlz) — warm-blooded animals that have hair or fur and usually give birth to live babies; female mammals produce milk to feed their young

marine (muh-REEN) — having to do with the ocean

mates (MAYTS) — animals that join with other animals to reproduce

migrate (MYE-grate) — to move to another area or climate at a particular time of year

parasites (PAIR-uh-sites) — animals or plants that live on or inside of another animal or plant

pectoral (PEK-tuh-ruhl) — related to or situated in the chest

pod (PAHD) — a group of certain kinds of sea animals, as in a pod of whales

predators (PRED-uh-turz) — animals that live by hunting other animals for food

school (SKOOL) — a group of fish or sea creatures swimming or feeding together

species (SPEE-sheez) — one of the groups into which animals and plants of the same genus are divided; members of the same species can mate and have offspring

warm-blooded (WARM-BLUHD-id) — having a warm body temperature that does not change, even if the temperature around is very hot or very cold

zooplankton (ZOH-uh-plank-tun) — small animals that live in saltwater

Habitat Map

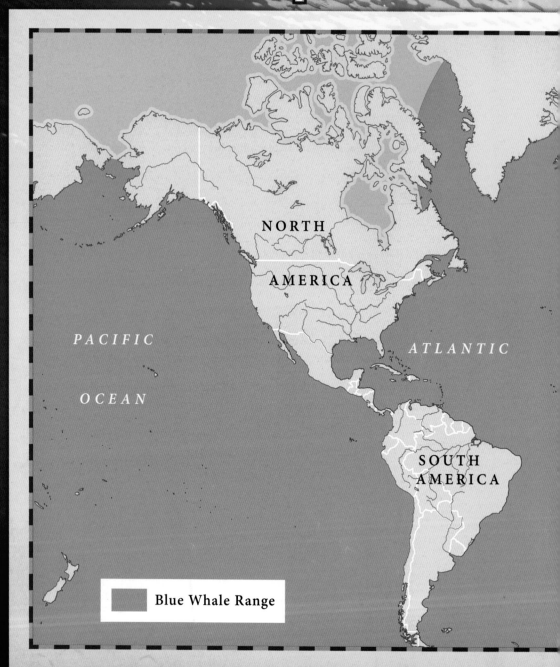

NORTH

AMERICA

PACIFIC

OCEAN

ATLANTIC

SOUTH
AMERICA

Blue Whale Range

ARCTIC OCEAN

EUROPE

ASIA

AFRICA

PACIFIC

OCEAN

OCEAN

INDIAN

OCEAN

AUSTRALIA

Find Out More

Books

Greenberg, Daniel A., and Nina Hess. *Whales*. New York: Marshall Cavendish Benchmark, 2010.

Hoyt, Erich. *Whale Rescue: Changing the Future for Endangered Wildlife*. Buffalo, NY: Firefly Books, 2005.

Johnson, Christina. *Blue Whales and Other Baleen Whales*. Chicago: World Book, 2005.

Portman, Michael. *Whales in Danger*. New York: Gareth Stevens, 2012.

Visit this Scholastic Web site for more information on blue whales:
www.factsfornow.scholastic.com
Enter the keywords **Blue Whales**

Index

Page numbers in *italics* indicate a photograph or map.

ancient species, *28*, 29

babies. *See* calves.
baleen plates, 6, 22, 29, 30
blowholes, 6, *8*, 9, 18, 29
blubber, 17, 21, 30, 37
Blue Whale Units (BWU), 34
body temperatures, *16*, 17
breathing, *8*, 9, 17, 18, 25

calves, 9, *24*, 25, 26
climate change, 37
colors, 6
communication, 18, 26, 38
conservation, 38, *40*, 41

diving, 6, 13, 14
dorsal fins, 6, 13

ears, 9, 18
endangered species, 34, 41
extinction, *28*, 29, 34, 41
eyes, 18, *19*

females, 9, *24*, 25, 26
fins. *See* dorsal fins; flippers; flukes.
fin whales, 29, 34
flippers, 6, 13, 29
flukes, 6, *12*, 13
food. *See* krill; milk.
fossils, *28*, 29

gestation period, 25
gray whales, 29

habitats, 10, *11*, *16*, 17, 33, 37, 41
hair, 9
harpoons, 30, 41
heads, 6, 13, *19*
heart, 17
hunting. *See* whaling industry.

jaws, 22

keratin, 22
killer whales. *See* orca whales.
krill, 6, 9, 10, *20*, 21, 22, *23*, 26, *27*, 37, 38

Larsen, Carl, 32, 33, 41
laws, 37, 41
lengths, 6, 13, 25
life spans, 41
lobtailing, 13

males, 26
mammals, 9, 17, 29
mating, 25, 26
migration, 10, 21, 25, 26, 38
milk, 9, 25

nostrils. *See* blowholes.

(Index continued)

orca whales, 14, *15*
oxygen, 9, 17

parasites, 37
people, *11*, 17, 22, 30, *31*, 32, 34, *35*,
   37, 38, *39*, 41
pods, 14, 26
pollution, 37, 41
population, 33, 34, 38
predators, 30, *31*, *32*, 34, *35*, 38

seasons, 10, 21, 25
senses, 18, 37
ships, 30, *31*, 37, 38
sizes, 6, 10, 13, 17, *19*, 25
skin, 13, 17
sleeping, 9

speeds, 14
suborders, 29
swimming, 9, 13, 14, *16*, 25

tails, 6, *12*, 13
tongues, 22
toothed whales, 29
tracking, 34, 38, *39*

U.S. Marine Mammal Protection Act,
   41

weight, 6, 10, 17, 25
whaling industry, 30, *31*, *32*, 34, *35*, 38
World War I, 33

zooplankton, *20*, 21

About the Author

Ruth Bjorklund lives on Bainbridge Island, near Seattle, Washington. She graduated with a master's degree in library science from the University of Washington and has written numerous books for children and teens. Most winters she travels to Baja California Sur and enjoys watching the gigantic "blows" of gray whales, humpbacks, and sometimes, but rarely, blue whales.